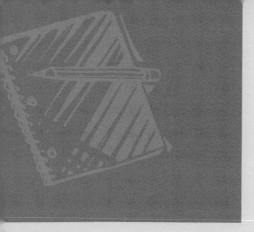

Keeping a notebook is the single best way I know to survive as a writer. It encourages you to pay attention to your world, inside and out. It serves as a container to keep together all the seeds you gather until you're ready to plant them. It gives you a quiet place to catch your breath and begin to write.

—Ralph Fletcher, *Breathing In, Breathing Out: Keeping a Writer's Notebook* (1996, 1)

Your notebook is a room of your own. It provides a safe place for you to ask:

What do I notice?

What do I care about?

What really matters?

What moves the deepest part of me?

What haunts me?

What do I want to remember—in my life, in this world—for the rest of my life?

What do I want to write about?

How might I begin?

—Ralph Fletcher, *Breathing In, Breathing Out: Keeping a Writer's Notebook* (1996, 3)

HEINEMANN ❖ PORTSMOUTH, NH

Expectations

To read voraciously for pleasure,
      because there are so many great books
To write or draw everything you think or feel or believe,
      because your thinking matters

                    —Linda Rief

Keeping Your Writer's-Reader's Notebook

Maintain Your:

◆ *Books I Am Currently Reading* List
◆ *Books I Want to Read* List
◆ *Ideas for Writing* List

Response Section

◆ To collect writing ideas and initial drafts of writing.

◆ To collect/respond to/react to/reflect on reading (books, magazines, instructions, other classes, etc.), writing, observations, and discoveries about yourself, others, and the world with _____ pages of writing, collected pictures, charts, cartoons, lists, drawings per week.

◆ To read for _____ each night, _____ times per week.

◆ To record _____ entries per week. An entry looks like this:

> Date
> <u>Title of Book</u> (or <u>Magazine</u> and "Article")
> Time spent reading, pages read

◆ To read with a writer's eye—what are you noticing/learning about writing from the writers you read?

◆ To collect at least *one poem per month,* glued into your *Writer's-Reader's Notebook (W-RN)* with an explanation of why you chose this poem and how it reflects you and your thinking at the moment.

Notes Section

◆ To record all notes given in class.

◆ To maintain a *Table of Contents* for these lessons/instructions, so you can easily find and use the information.

Vocabulary Section

◆ To "find" at least _____ words per week that are new or unknown (from reading, listening, talking, in or out of school). These are words you'd like to begin to use in your speaking and writing.

◆ To write each word in the vocab section of this *W-RN* in the sentence in which you found the word and with the appropriate definition (based on the context of the sentence) written in your own words.

◆ To look for and record each new context in which you discover the same word again (this counts as a new word: same word in new context) with the appropriate definition.

Spelling Matters Section

◆ To maintain *Spelling rules* and *Personal Spelling Lists* (the last section in your *W-RN*).

◆ When given the correct spelling of words on your pre-final draft in language arts or any other class, to write those words under the rule that applies to their spelling, or through usage, or on your *Personal Spelling List* when they are the exception to all the rules.

Books I Am Currently Reading

TITLE	NO. OF PAGES	AUTHOR	DATE BEGUN	DATE FINISHED	DEGREE OF DIFFICULTY *easy, just right, hard*	RATING 1 2 3 4 5 BEST ONE-WORD DESCRIPTION

Books I Want to Read

Title and Author	Recommended By

Reason to Read

Title and Author	Recommended By

Reason to Read

Title and Author	Recommended By

Reason to Read

Title and Author	Recommended By

Reason to Read

Title and Author	Recommended By

Reason to Read

Title and Author	Recommended By

Reason to Read

Title and Author	Recommended By

Reason to Read

Title and Author	Recommended By

Reason to Read

Title and Author	Recommended By

Reason to Read

Ideas for Writing

What I Want to Write _____

_____

How I Came Up with the Idea _____

_____

What I Want to Write _____

_____

How I Came Up with the Idea _____

_____

What I Want to Write _____

_____

How I Came Up with the Idea _____

_____

What I Want to Write _____

_____

How I Came Up with the Idea _____

_____

What I Want to Write _____

_____

How I Came Up with the Idea _____

_____

Response

Most of the basic material a writer works with is acquired before the age of fifteen.

—Willa Cather, From *Shoptalk* (Donald Murray 1990, 16)

Combining word and image in my journal is a particular kind of gathering together that's really important to me. . . . There's something about the attempt to draw that makes the difference. It can be hard to talk ourselves out of that controlling voice that judges the marks we make. When I get back home from drawing and flip through my sketchbook, I'm always surprised that my drawings look as good as they do. The real work is quieting the voice that says "I can't do it," and just getting down to observing, drawing, and learning. I end up surprising myself.

—Barbara Bash, author and illustrator, from *Speaking of Journals* (Paula Graham, 1999, 6, 9)

_____

_____

_____

_____

_____

_____

_____

_____

_____

_____

_____

_____

_____

_____

_____

_____

_____

_____

_____

_____

_____

_____

_____

_____

I first got the idea of keeping a journal because I wanted to save some of the funny things my kids did. My son Keenan once asked: "Does God have armpits?"... Now I use journals not so much as a source of ideas, but more a key to memories.

—Graham Salisbury, author, from *Speaking of Journals* (Paula Graham, 1999, 38–39)

Be a sponge . . . alive to the world . . . develop the habit of paying attention
to the little pictures and images of the world you might otherwise ignore.

—Ralph Fletcher, *A Writer's Notebook* (1996, 45)

A writer's notebook . . . gives you a place to write down what makes you angry or sad or amazed, to write down what you noticed and don't want to forget, to record exactly what your grandmother whispered in your ear before she said goodbye for the last time.

—Ralph Fletcher, *A Writer's Notebook* (1996, 3)

The significance of my journal is that it leads me back instantly to who I was. I can become the twelve-year-old kid again, worry about his complexion and his glasses that were heavy and kept sliding down his nose when he was hot, getting gangly with big feet and knees.

—David Harrison, poet, from *Speaking of Journals* (Paula Graham, 1999, 13–14)

It is a writer's job to act as a witness to the world, to remind us all to stay awake.

—Georgia Heard, *Writing Toward Home* (1995, 91)

You can't write a journal if you're thinking of an audience first rather than yourself.
A journal at its best should be a completely free and open conversation with yourself.

—James Cross Giblin, author, from *Speaking of Journals* (Paula Graham, 1999, 49)

Journal writing frees me up to explore my fictional characters. It brings me to a human foundation so I can see the characters as fully human, especially when I have to write evil characters. There are more sides to them and that's about knowing and understanding my own everyday actions when I don't behave in the best manner.

—Jacqueline Woodson, author, from *Speaking of Journals* (Paula Graham, 1999, 65)

Becoming a better writer is going to help you become
a better reader, and that is the real payoff.

—Anne Lamott, *Bird by Bird* (1994, 10)

The point of a notebook [journal] is to jumpstart your mind.

—John Gregory Dunn, from *Shoptalk* (Donald Murray, 1990, 83)

Donald Murray once wrote . . . "It takes forty gallons of maple sap to make one gallon of maple syrup." Maple sap is mostly water. To make syrup, you've got to boil off that water. Much of what you write in your writer's notebook is like that water sap . . . You have to boil off lots of water in order to make the syrup of your writing.

—Ralph Fletcher, *A Writer's Notebook* (1996, 120)

I took a hiatus from work and decided to go out each day and simply enjoy nature. . . . I just let nature flow into me and onto the pages of my journal. In those seven months I learned so much more about the landscape, and by adhering to a rigorous schedule I found myself drawing nearer and nearer to the animals.

Thinking is not a replacement for living. I don't like nurturing the concept in children that if they read about an eagle, it somehow equals seeing one. I'm always hopeful that teachers and parents will stress the importance of the smallest personal experience over the most extravagant and most beautifully written account of something.

—Jim Arnosky, author and artist, from *Speaking of Journals* (Paula Graham, 1999, 78, 81)

Writing draws out of memory what can't be recalled any other way. . . . As you notice more, what you notice increases. . . . Awareness makes writing possible . . . writing increases awareness.

—Donald Murray, *Shoptalk* (1990, 14–15)

To become a good writer, you need to do three things. Read a lot, listen well and deeply, and write a lot. And don't think too much. Just enter the heat of words and sounds and colored sensations and keep your pen moving across the page.

—Natalie Goldberg, _Writing Down the Bones_ (1986, 54)

I tell [kids] that this [journal] is the single most important book that they will write. Whether they become poets or novelists, or better business letter writers. . . . At the end of their lives the books they are going to be most satisfied with are their journals.

When you write about yourself, observations, activities, speculations against those activities, and other people's lives, you're expanding who you are, stretching the boundaries of who you are, and you're becoming an ever-larger person. You're expanding your territories. You're Hannibal crossing the Alps.

—Jack Gantos, author, from *Speaking of Journals* (Paula Graham, 1999, 110–111)

Reading and writing allow you to express your own feelings while learning about someone else's.
—Troy, eighth grader

Our life is imprinted on our brain, but we can't pull it all up. The journal is like a fishhook you can drop in your brain and pull out memories very efficiently. The sights and sounds and the smells are going to come rushing back to you. . . . When I read a sentence in my journal it can bring up a whole day in my mind.

—Bruce Coville, author, from *Speaking of Journals* (Paula Graham, 1999, 190–192)

Like an investigative reporter, Holbrook trains her eye on the details of her world. She searches out sights, sounds, and smells—a squished squirrel, a clanking flagpole, the ripe air of zoo cages—and translates these images into notes and phrases. She dashes them down on index cards she carries in her wallet. Back home, she transfers these observations into her journal, where they incubate, sometimes for years, until she revisits them and spins them into poems.

—About Sara Holbrook, poet, from *Speaking of Journals* (Paula Graham, 1999, 145–146)

No surprise for the writer, no surprise for the reader. For me the initial delight is in the surprise of remembering something I didn't know I knew.

—Robert Frost, from *Shoptalk* (Donald Murray 1990, 101)

What I learned quickly, and what kept me writing so intensely, was being able to look back, even only a couple of weeks after an entry and say, "Well, I got through that. I'm still struggling, I'm still frustrated, I'm still confused and sad about this stuff, but I got through it."

It was simple things like losing a girlfriend or arguing with my parents, not doing very well in school or being frustrated with how I did in a race. To me these were life-shaping events. At the time I had three things that kept me kind of sane. One was the journal.

—Rich Wallace, author, from *Speaking of Journals* (Paula Graham, 1999, 172–173)

The two most useful things any writer can do is read widely and keep notebooks, writing on a regular basis. William Stafford, my favorite poet, believed that we must train ourselves to become more alert and attentive to all the messages, signs, and images around us, and that keeping an ongoing, regular notebook was one of the best exercises for maintaining alertness.

—Naomi Shihab Nye, author and poet, from *Speaking of Journals* (Paula Graham 1999, 206)

You have to imagine yourself inside the book, with the characters, feeling and seeing what they do as if you were really there. Not just reading words. Reading is painting a picture of what the author is trying to tell you.

—Shannon, eighth grader

Sometimes you've got to read something that contains the interest
that fits you like a glove. This reading for me is Sports Illustrated.

—Mike, eighth grader

_____

_____

_____

_____

_____

_____

_____

_____

_____

_____

_____

_____

_____

_____

_____

_____

_____

_____

_____

_____

The best book I've ever read so far is <u>The Cage</u> *by Ruth Minsky-Sender. The book was so good because... it kept me reading, it made me realize how good my life is, and how lucky I am.*

—Kyung, eighth grader

Long before I wrote stories, I listened for stories. Listening for them is something more acute than listening to them.

—Eudora Welty, *One Writer's Beginnings* (1984, 14)

Notes

Table of Contents

(Date all notes as they are given in class.)

PAGE NO.	DATE	TOPIC
1.		
2.		
3.		
4.		
5.		
6.		
7.		
8.		
9.		
10.		
11.		
12.		

PAGE NO.	DATE	TOPIC
13.		
14.		
15.		
16.		
17.		
18.		
19.		
20.		
21.		
22.		
23.		
24.		

Vocabulary

In her published journal, *A Circle of Quiet*, author Madeleine L'Engle says:

The more limited our language is, the more limited we are; the more limited the lit-
erature we give our children, the more limited their capacity to respond, and there-
fore, in their turn, to create. The more our vocabulary is controlled, the less we will
be able to think for ourselves. We do think in words, and the fewer words we know,
the more restricted our thoughts. As our vocabulary expands, so does our power to
think. (1972, 149).

You are to find and write down _____ *words per week* to add to the vocabulary words I will
give you. Write *the sentence in which you find or hear the word, underline the word, and jot down the
definition* that best fits the word based on the sentence in which it appears. Choose words that
intrigue you, words that you really want to know. Date each week.

(Remember, definitions are numbered in the dictionary beginning with most common use of a
word, which may not be the best meaning for the way your word is used in the sentence.)

Extra Credit:
- Find and write down the etymology, or history, of the word (usually found at the end of the
  entry in the dictionary).
- Draw a sketch or picture that shows your understanding of the word.
- Write your own sentence using the word appropriately and giving it a context that lets us know
  you understand the use of the word.

Where do you find or hear the words? In your reading! In newspapers or magazines! From
teachers, parents, peers! On TV! Everywhere!

Here is an example of how to write down the vocabulary words you want to remember:

9/18

He used his heels to **goad** the brown pony up and out of the gully Sanota
had led them to; ahead Magpie caught the sun and his long black hair
shone like a raven's wing in the light. (Paulsen, <u>Canyons</u>, 1990, 18)

Goad (v) = to coax, persuade, prod, urge

Here is an example of how to earn extra credit:

Spelling Matters

There is little point in learning to spell if you have little intention of writing.

—Frank Smith

Spelling matters, especially in your final drafts. You want a reader to understand clearly what you are thinking and saying. Standard spelling helps us understand what a writer means.

However, there is no reason to continually worry about spelling correctly in your first drafts. Getting ideas on paper and crafting those ideas in the best order with the strongest, most compelling words matter the most. When you are satisfied with what you've said and how you've said it, you can carefully edit for the correct conventions of language, in order to give your reader clear directions on how to read it. This includes correct spelling.

One of the ways you might learn to strengthen your spelling is to organize the words that give you difficulty under the rules that guide their spelling. This will help you understand patterns of spelling with which you may be having trouble. Organizing the words this way will help you remember how these particular words are guided by specific rules. As you notice, figure out, and receive corrections to the spelling of words, add them to this list. Notice, however, that many words in English might not fit any of these categories; you should add those words to your *Personal Spelling List.*

(Spelling rules adapted from Sebranek, P., V. Meyer, and D. Kemper. 1993. *Writers Inc.* Lexington, MA: D. C. Heath and Co.)

Spelling Rule 1: Write *i* before *e*, except after *c*, or when sounded like *a*, as in *neighbor* and *weigh*

Examples of *i before e:* *friend, believe, view, achieve, belief, thief, grief, chief, yield*

Examples of *except after c:* *receive, receipt, conceited*

Examples of *ei sounding like long a:* *neighbor, weigh, reign, sleigh*

Exceptions to the above rules: *neither, either, weird, their, foreign, seize, leisure, height*

Spelling Rule 2: When **a one-syllable word** (*bat*) **ends in a consonant** (*t*) **preceded by one vowel** (*a*), **double the final consonant before adding a suffix that begins with a vowel** (*batting*).

Examples: *bat—batting; sum—summary; god—goddess*

When **a multisyllable word** (*control*) **ends in a consonant** (*l*) **preceded by one vowel** (*o*), **and the accent is on the last syllable** (*con trol'*), **and the suffix begins with a vowel** (*ing*), **the same rule holds true**: **double the final consonant** (*controlling*).

Examples: *forget—forgettable; prefer—preferred; begin—beginning; admit—admittance*

Spelling Rule 3: If a word ends with a silent *e*, drop the *e* before adding a suffix that begins with a vowel. Do not drop the *e* when the suffix begins with a consonant.

Examples:

state—stating—statement
like—liking—likeness
use—using—useful
nine—ninety—nineteen
hope—hoping—hopeless
use—using—usable—useful
write—writing

Exceptions:

judge—judgment; true—truly; argue—argument; nine—ninth

Spelling Rule 4: When *y* is the last letter in a word and the *y* is preceded by a consonant, change the *y* to *i* before adding any suffix, except those beginning with *i*.

Examples: *fry—fries; hurry—hurried; try—tried—tries; lady—ladies; happy—happiness—happiest; beauty—beautiful*

When forming the **plural of a word that ends with a *y* that is preceded by a vowel, add *s*.**

Examples: *toy—toys; play—plays; monkey—monkeys*

Spelling Rule 5: For words ending in *c*, insert *k* before *e*, *i*, or *y* endings to retain the hard sound.

Examples: *picnic—picnicked; panic—panicked*

Usage

Usage refers to using the correct spelling depending on its meaning. Many words in English have different meanings but similar spelling. The differences may be how they are used, or they may be homonyms.

Homonyms may be homographs (words that are spelled the same way but have different meanings, such as *bear*, the animal, and *bear*, to support) or homophones (words that sound the same but have different spellings and meanings, such as *bear*, the animal, and *bare*, naked or plain).

Examples

Here are some examples of words that change spelling based on how they are *used*. Please write the way each of these words is *used* next to it. As you find others that you need to remember, add the words and their usage to your list. Writing a phrase that shows how to use the word helps you remember it.

their

they're

there

accept

except

it's

its

then

than

Personal Spelling List

Many words in English don't fit under any of the preceding rules. Words on this list should come from your misspelled words on written work, including those from other classes. Writing those words here, and referring to this list, will help you remember the correct spellings as you use these words again.